40 HAPPE

Written By:
Herbert Kavet

Illustrated By:
Martin Riskin

Manufactured in the United States of America

30 29 28 27 26 25 24 23 22 21 20 19 18 17 16 15 14 13 12 11 10 9 8 7

Ivory Tower Publishing Co., Inc.
125 Walnut St., Watertown, MA 02172
Telephone #: (617) 923-1111   Fax #: (617) 923-8839

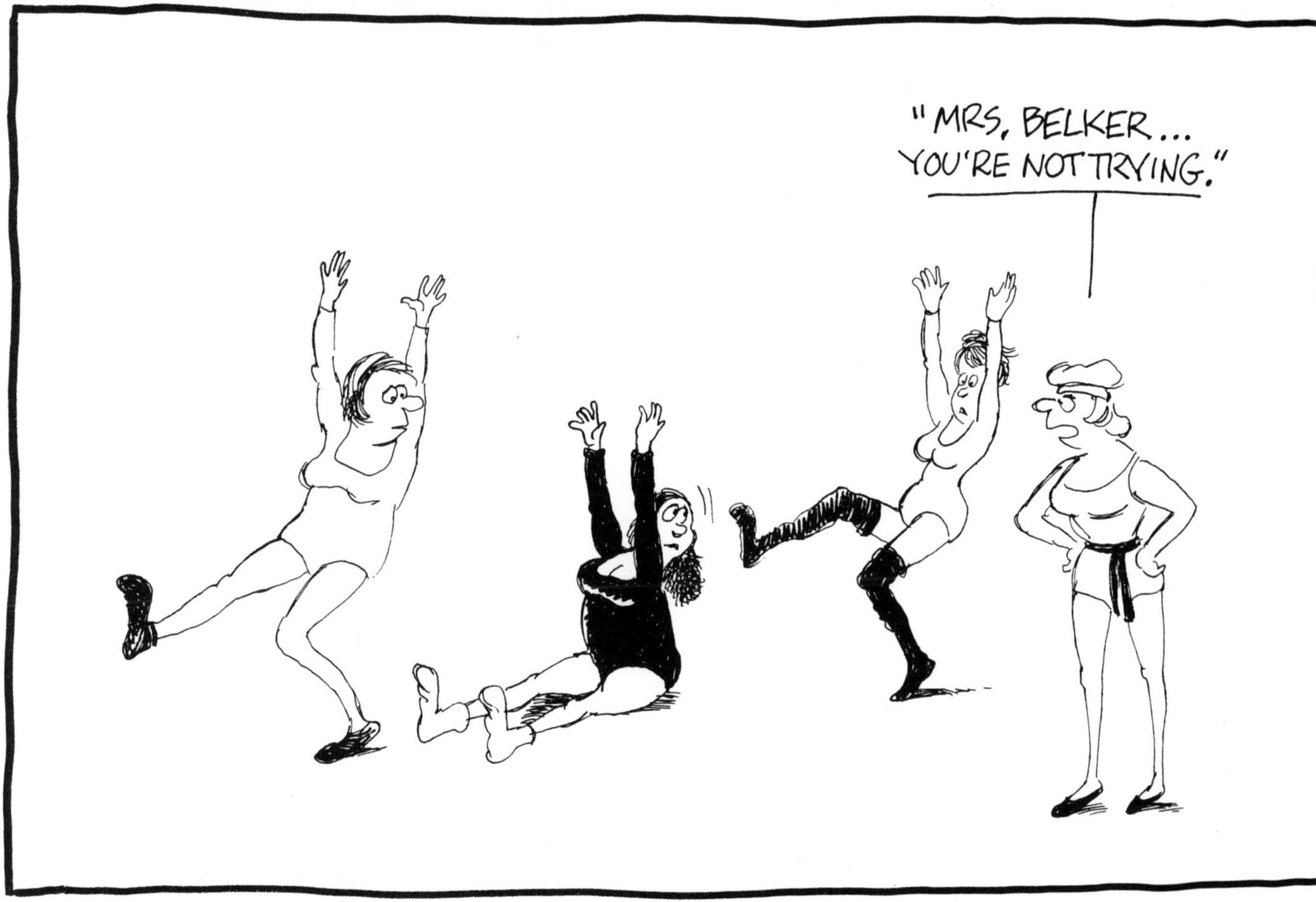
"MRS. BELKER...
YOU'RE NOT TRYING."

THE FIRST GRAY HAIR.

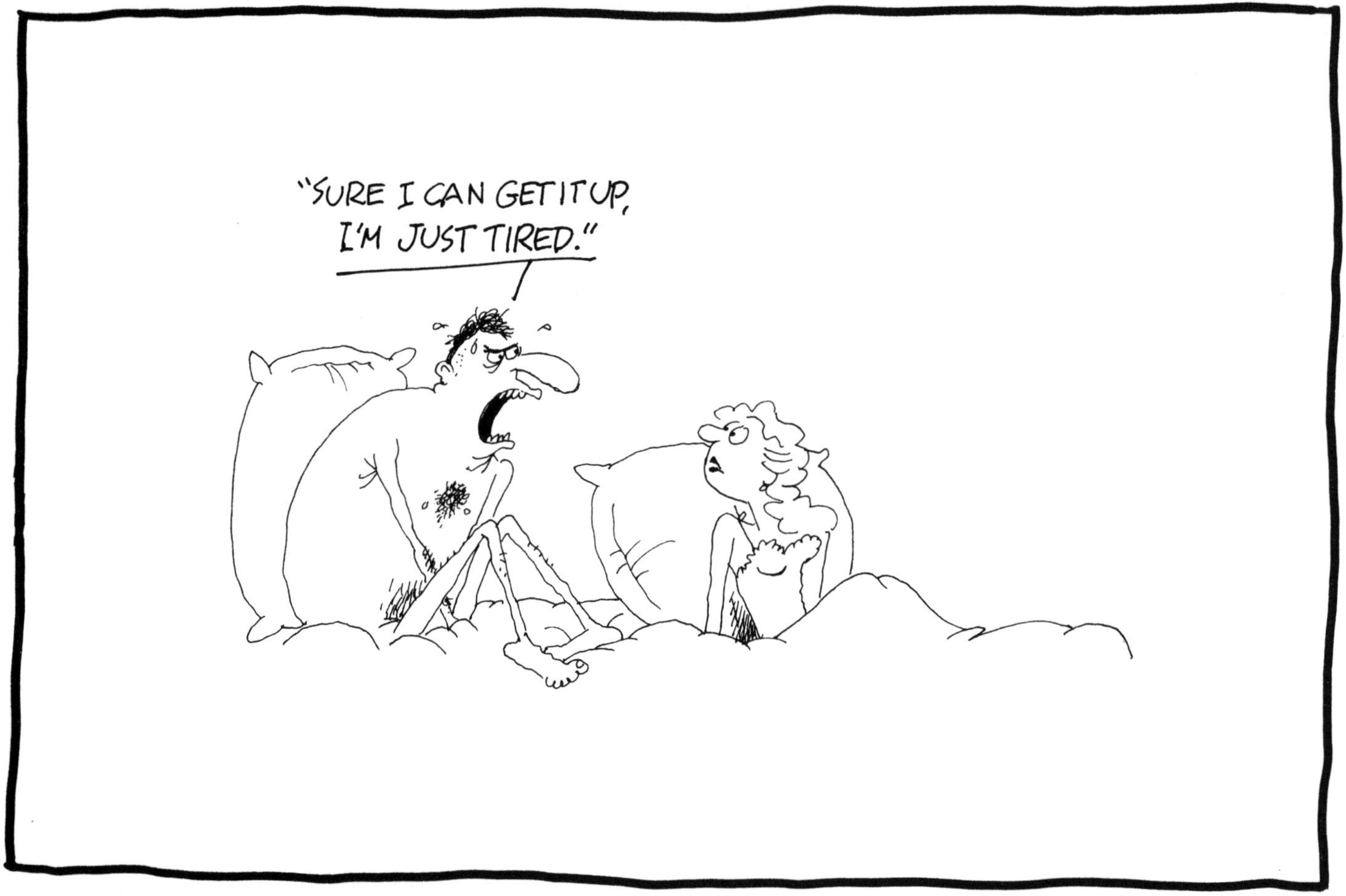
"SURE I CAN GET IT UP, I'M JUST TIRED."

FEAR IS THE FIRST TIME YOU CAN'T DO IT TWICE.
TERROR IS THE SECOND TIME YOU CAN'T DO IT ONCE.

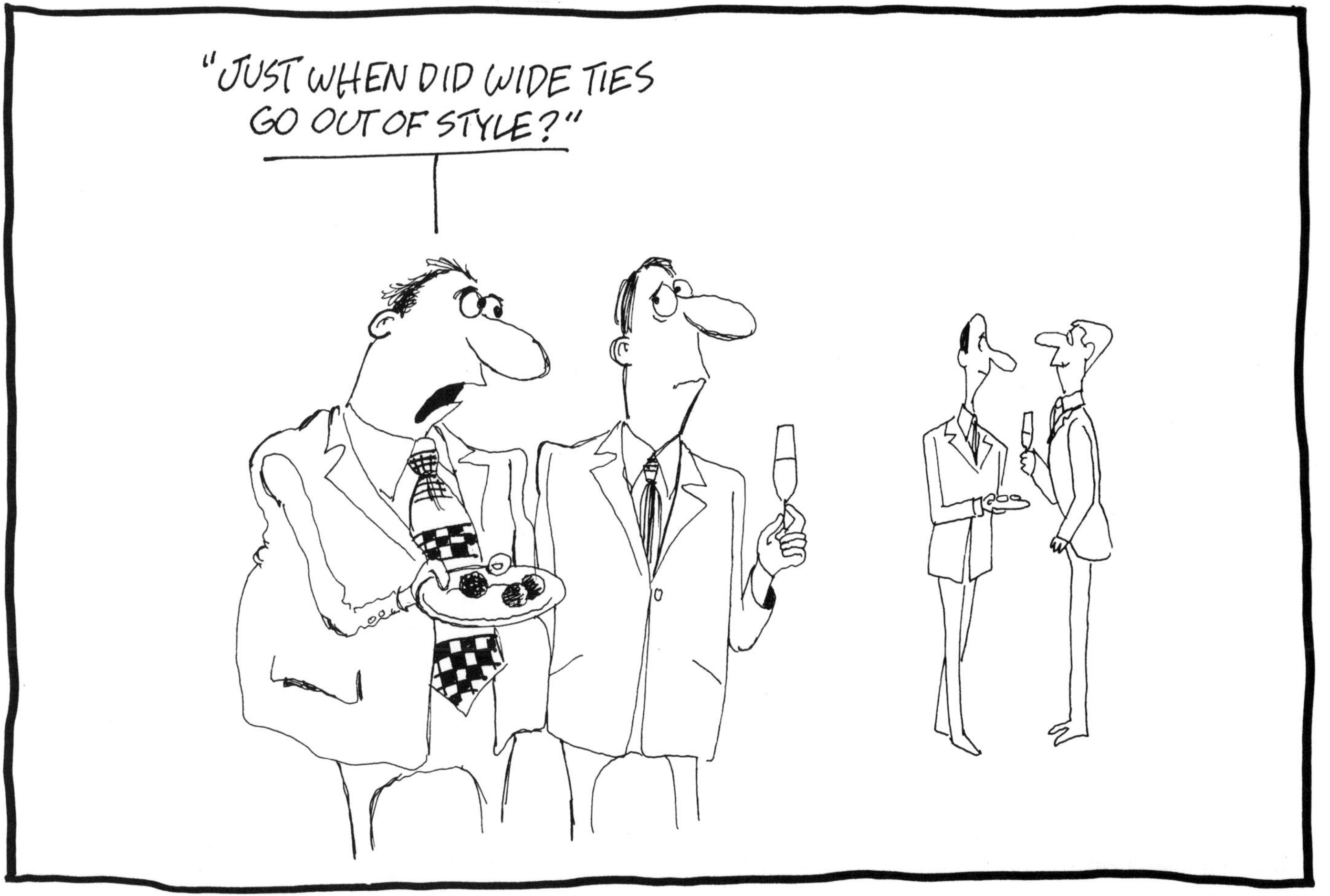
"JUST WHEN DID WIDE TIES GO OUT OF STYLE?"

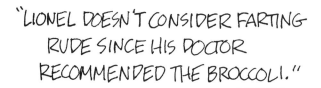

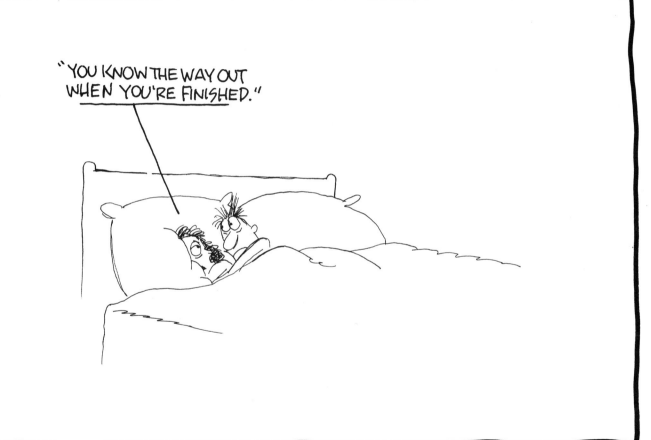

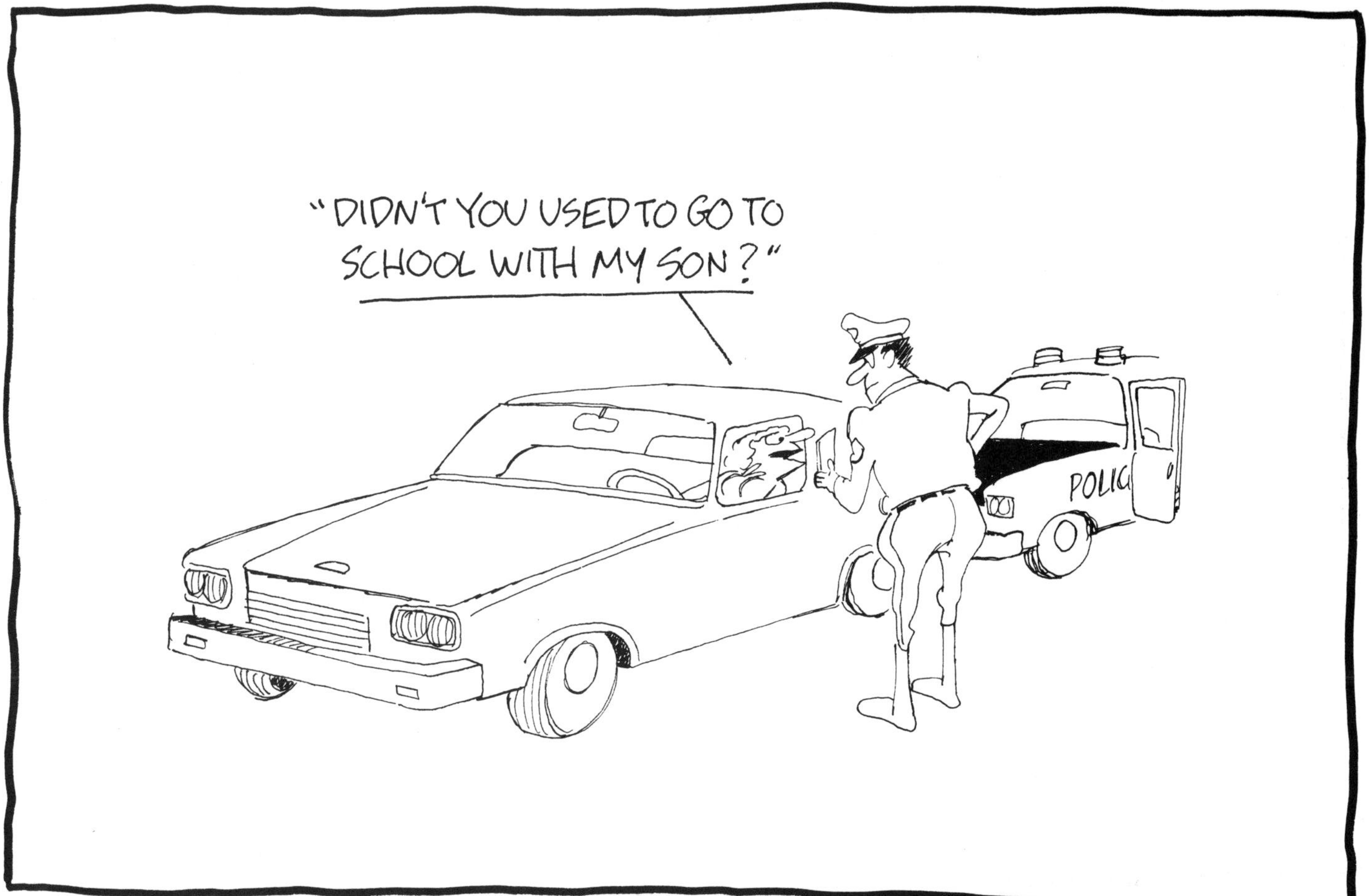
"DIDN'T YOU USED TO GO TO SCHOOL WITH MY SON?"
POLIC

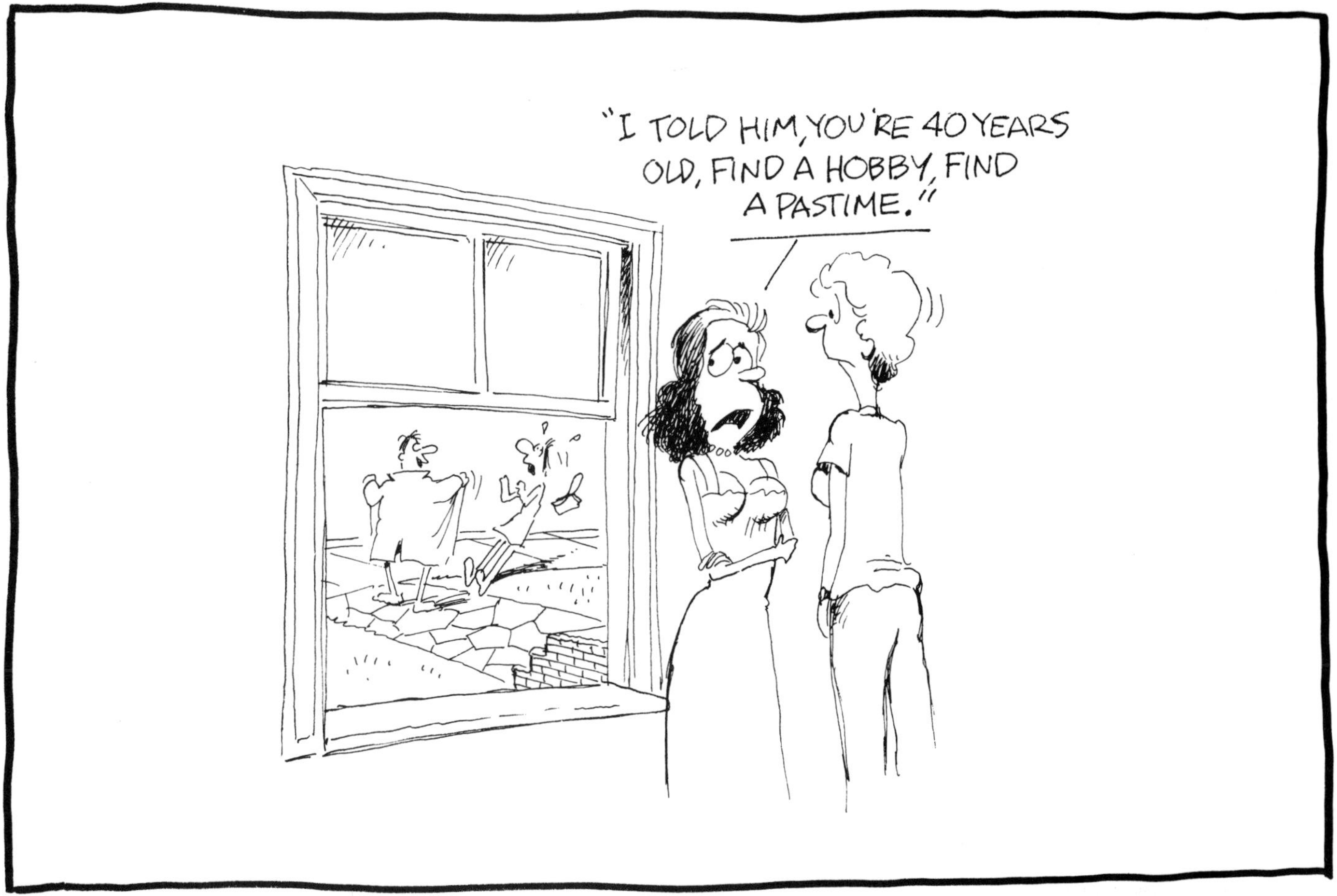
"I TOLD HIM, YOU'RE 40 YEARS OLD, FIND A HOBBY, FIND A PASTIME."

"FRELLMAN DRESSES FOR COMFORT"

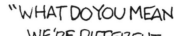

Other books we publish are available at many fine stores. If you can't find them, send directly to us. $7.00 postpaid

2400-How To Have Sex On Your Birthday. Finding a partner, special birthday sex positions and much more.

2402-Confessions From The Bathroom. There are things in this book that happen to all of us that none of us ever talk about, like the Gas Station Dump, the Corn Niblet Dump and more.

2403-The Good Bonking Guide. A great new term for doing "you know what". Bonking in the dark, bonking all night long, improving your bonking, and everything else you ever wanted to know.

2407-40 Happens. When being out of prune juice ruins your whole day and you realize anyone with the energy to do it on a weeknight must be a sex maniac.

2408-30 Happens. When you take out a lifetime membership at your health club, and you still wonder when the baby fat will finally disappear.

2409-50 Happens. When you remember when "made in Japan" meant something that didn't work, and you can't remember what you went to the top of the stairs for.

2411-The Geriatric Sex Guide. It's not his mind that needs expanding; and you're in the mood now, but by the time you're naked, you won't be!

2412-Golf Shots. What excuses to use to play through first, ways to distract your opponent, and when and where a true golfer is willing to play.

2414-60 Happens. When your kids start to look middle-aged, when software is some kind of comfortable underwear, and when your hearing is perfect if everyone would just stop mumbling.

2416-The Absolutely Worst Fart Book. The First Date Fart, The Lovers' Fart, The Doctor's Exam Room Fart and more.

2417-Women Over 30 Are Better Because... Their nightmares about exams are starting to fade and their handbags can sustain life for about a week with no outside support whatsoever.

2418-9 Months In The Sac. Pregnancy through the eyes of the baby, such as: why do pregnant women have to go to the bathroom as soon as they get to the store, and why does baby start doing aerobics when it's time to sleep?

2419-Cucumbers Are Better Than Men Because... Cucumbers are always ready when you are and cucumbers will never hear "yes, yes" when you're saying "NO, NO."

2421-Honeymoon Guide. From The Advantages Of Undressing With The Light On (it's easier to undo a bra) to What Men Want Most (being allowed to sleep right afterwards without having to talk about love).

2422-Eat Yourself Healthy. Calories only add up if the food is consumed at a table—snacking doesn't count. Green M&M's are full of the same vitamins found in broccoli and more useful eating information your mother never told you.

2423-Is There Sex After 40? She liked you better when the bulge above your waist used to be the bulge in your trousers. He thinks wife-swapping means getting someone else to cook for you.

2424-Is There Sex After 50? Going to bed early just means a chance to catch up on your reading or watch a little extra TV, and you actually miss trying to make love quietly so as not to wake the kids.

2425-Women Over 40 Are Better Because... They realize that no matter how many sit-ups and leg raises they do, they cannot recapture their 17-year-old figures—but they can find something attractive in any 21-year-old guy.

2426-Women Over 50 Are Better Because... More reasons why women over 50 are better: They will be amused if you take them parking, and they know that being alone is better than being with someone they don't like.

2427-You Know You're Over The Hill When... All the stories of your youth have bored most acquaintances several times over. You're resigned to being slightly overweight after trying every diet that has come along in the last 15 years.

2428-Beer Is Better Than Women Because (Part II)... A beer doesn't get upset if you call it by the wrong name; and after several beers, you can roll over and go to sleep without having to talk about love.

2429-Married To A Computer. You fondle it daily, you keep in touch when you're travelling and you stare at it a lot without understanding it.

2430-Is There Sex After 30? Parking isn't as much fun as it was in high school. He thinks foreplay means parading around nude in front of the mirror, holding his stomach in; and she has found that the quickest way to get rid of an unwanted date is to start talking about commitment.

2431-Happy Birthday You Old Fart! You spend less and less time between visits to a toilet, your back goes out more than you do and you leave programming the VCR to people under 25.

2432-Big Weenies. Why some people have big weenies while other people have teenie weenies; as well as the kinds of men who possess a member, a rod and a wang—and more!

2433-Games You Can Play With Your Pussy. Why everyone should have a pussy; how to give a pussy a bath (grease the sides of the tub so it can't claw its way out); and more!.

2434-Sex And Marriage. What wives want out of marriage (romance, respect and a Bloomingdale's Charge Card); what husbands want out of marriage (to be allowed to go to sleep after sex).

2435-Diapers, Doo-Doo & Diddlypoop Baby's First Year. How much will it cost, the secrets of midnight feedings, do diapers really cause leprosy and other vital info for parents.

2436-How To Love A New Yorker. You love a New Yorker by pretending to understand their accent, sharing a parking space, getting it for them wholesale and realizing they look at "Out of Towners" as a supplemental source of income.

2437-The Retirement Book. Brings the retiree up to date on Early Bird Specials, finding their bifocals, dressing like a retired person and remembering important things like paying for the book.

2438-Dog Farts. They do it under the table, in front of the TV, on the way to the vet and after devouring some horrible animal they caught in the yard. This book describes them all.

2439-Handling His Midlife Crisis. By treating him like a child when he wants to feel young again, consoling him when he goes from bikinis to boxer shorts and making sure he has something green with each meal besides Heineken beer.

2440-How To Love A Texan. You love a Texan by agreeing that their chili is just a mite hot, humoring them when they refer to their half acre as a ranch and rushing to help when their belt buckle sets off a security alarm.

Ivory Tower Publishing Co., Inc., 125 Walnut St., P.O. Box 9132, Watertown, MA 02272-9132   Tel: (617) 923-1111